THINKING OUT
LOUD

THINKING OUT

LOUD

THE WIT AND WISDOM OF
Lemmy

appreciated and deconstructed by
PAUL BRANNIGAN

First published in 2009 by Aurum Press Ltd
7 Greenland Street, London NW1 0ND
www.aurumpress.co.uk

A catalogue record for this book is available from
the British Library.

ISBN 978 1 84513 485 3

10 9 8 7 6 5 4 3 2 1
2013 2012 2010 2011 2009

Text design in Helvetica by Roger Hammond
Printed by MPG Books Ltd, Bodmin, Cornwall

Contents

Introduction

'He is God. He is the reason. He is the last man standing and no one even comes close. That guy is a true rock 'n' roller. Everyone else is just trying.'

Dave Grohl (Foo Fighters/Nirvana), 2002

People say you can only depend on two things in life: death and taxes. Make that three: death, taxes and Lemmy. Nations may rise and fall, seas may ebb and flow, fashions may change but Lemmy remains an absolute, a constant, a rock. He is one of the last true musical outlaws, a genuine rock 'n' roll rebel, a hard-livin', hard-rockin', hell-raisin' hero to millions. Lesser men have had their faces carved into Mount Rushmore.

You will know the man born Ian Fraser

Kilmister best as the face, voice, heart,
soul and balls of Motörhead, the great
British rock 'n' roll institution he has fronted
since 1975. Once officially recognised as
the loudest band in the world, Motörhead
remain one of the most uncompromising –
and uncompromised – acts around.
Named after a slang term for amphetamine
abusers, Lemmy's band deal in raw,
raucous, fast and furious primal rock 'n'
roll, ripped to the tits on Jack Daniel's
bourbon, Marlboro cigarettes and the
cheapest, nastiest industrial-strength
speed. At one point – back in the summer
of 1981, when their live album *No Sleep
'Til Hammersmith* (featuring bad-ass
boogie anthems such as 'Overkill',
'Bomber' and the breathless, deathless
'Ace of Spades') debuted at No. 1 in the
national charts – Motörhead were not only

the noisiest band in the UK, but also the most popular. But Motörhead's importance and influence cannot be measured purely in commercial terms: for over 30 years their name – and that of their redoubtable leader – has been a by-word for attitude, integrity, honesty and a stubborn, intransigent belief in doing things their own way. For three generations of Motörhead fans – and rock legends such as James Hetfield from Metallica, Dave Grohl from Foo Fighters and former Guns N' Roses guitarist Slash can be counted among that number – Lemmy is the phrase 'fuck you' made flesh and wrapped in skin-tight, genital-constricting black leather.

But that's only half the story. Beyond the two-dimensional rock 'n' roll gunslinger caricature, Lemmy is a fascinating, multi-faceted character: an English gentleman in love with the works of P.G. Wodehouse, a keen horseman, a diligent historical scholar, a collector of military memorabilia, animal skulls . . . and Kinder Egg toys. He's the son of a preacher man, a father of two, an outspoken anti-heroin campaigner, a stickler for old-fashioned manners. And, beyond that, he's a philosopher and sage for our times, blithely dispensing aphorisms with the benign wisdom of an elder statesman who's seen mankind at its most base and its most noble . . . quite possibly while on the road in the US supporting Ozzy Osbourne.

I had Christmas dinner with Lemmy, for a feature for heavy metal bible *Kerrang!*, some ten years ago. Strictly speaking it wasn't Christmas, and strictly speaking it didn't actually involve dinner either, as the great man waved away his roast turkey and sprouts, opting to stick with his traditional diet of (large) Jack Daniel's whisky and Coke, and forcefully suggesting that everyone else at the table should follow suit. But it was a memorable occasion, nonetheless. Lemmy chatted up the waitresses – one of whom greeted him with a raised eyebrow and the saucy line, 'And what will you be having, big boy?' – charmed fellow diners with a string of unprintable, possibly libellous anecdotes and scrawled a note to Santa on the back of a Hard Rock Café napkin requesting a bow and arrows, a Viking ship and a new cowboy hat. Sadly, we never heard if Santa came through for him. Sharp-witted, sarcastic, cantankerous and blunt, he was fabulous company, with an opinion on *everything*, whether you cared to hear it or not. If only all rock stars had a fraction of his charisma . . .

'I know a lot of rock 'n' roll personalities, and the ones I admire, the ones I'm drawn towards, are the ones that are the real deal,' says guitar hero Slash in the online trailer for the upcoming Lemmy movie, unfussily and snappily titled *Lemmy: The Movie*. 'People who live, sleep and breathe rock 'n' roll, the lifestyle and the attitude. There's only a handful of guys who are still alive who represent that. And Lemmy represents that to me.'

Everyone knows Lemmy, the man, the myth, the monster of rock. He is a national treasure, a force of nature, a legend. And this is his outspoken, fearless philosophy of life, warts and all . . .

Lemmy
on Motörhead

In the Spring of 1975 Lemmy was living out his rock 'n' roll dreams, touring America as the bassist in tripped-out space rockers Hawkwind. Then disaster struck. Crossing the Canadian border, the band's tour bus was raided by police and their bass player was arrested for cocaine possession (a charge subsequently thrown out when the drug turned out to be speed). After a night in jail, Lemmy was freed on bail and flew to Toronto to rejoin the band . . . who promptly sacked him after the show. He returned to London bitter, broke and out for revenge. Within weeks he'd formed a new band, named after the final song he'd written in Hawkwind. The name of that band? Motörhead.

THINKING OUT LOUD

On Hawkwind

'We were fucking fierce. We'd dose the audience with acid, lock the doors so they couldn't leave, then send them into epileptic fits with subsonic frequencies and strobes. Those were the days.' **2009**

. . .

On the concept behind Motörhead

'It'll be the dirtiest rock 'n' roll band in the world. If we moved in next door your lawn would die.' **1975**

'I know, intellectually, there was a time when I wasn't in Motörhead, but I can't actually remember it.' **2002**

'In another age, I would've run away and joined the circus, but, seeing as how it's this one, I joined a rock 'n' roll band. I think it's one of the great lives left.' **1999**

. . .

On being talked out of calling the band Bastard

'My manager pointed out that we probably wouldn't get a lot of *Top of the Pops* coverage, so I bent to his superior intellect.' **2005**

On Motörhead's early ambitions

'I just wanted to offend people's parents and be that band they feared, and that they thought their daughter was on her knees in the tour bus with.' **2000**

'I hope to have a very bad effect on people. Motörhead are supposed to make people wonder what's the next bad thing that will happen to them. Life is about brief periods of bliss followed by long periods of depression, angst and brutality.' **1999**

. . .

On Motörhead's sound
'We wanted to be like the MC5 crossed with Elvis Presley. But I haven't got the high notes he's got.' **2002**

'It's the soundtrack to WWIII.' **2008**

'Nobody's gonna be eating chicken out of a basket when we're up there.' **1997**

'To change our sound would be prostitution.' **2005**

On being asked by a Swedish reporter, 'If you played here again in ten years, how would you sound?'

'Same but louder.'

. . .

On his trademark rumbling bass sound

'I just turn it up really loud and hit it really hard!' **2003**

. . .

On suggestions that he's a 'difficult' boss

'It's not that hard to work with me, you just have to agree with everything I say.' **2007**

. . .

THINKING OUT LOUD

On Motörhead's best known song, 'Ace of Spades'

'It's clothed my back for the last 20 years.'
1998

'I sang "Eight of Spades" for five years and nobody noticed. That will show you how much attention people pay to the bloody vocals.' **1996**

. . .

Always destined to be a band that polarised opinion, Motörhead were once dubbed 'the best worst band in the world' in a poll conducted by weekly music magazine *NME*. If Lemmy was wholly untroubled by this back-handed 'tribute' – 'It was only the NME, which is a shit paper to start with' – he was no less worked up a few years later when Motörhead's live album, *No Sleep 'Til Hammersmith*, debuted at No. 1 in the UK album chart in the summer of 1981. Upon receiving an early morning phone call in his New York hotel room informing him of the achievement, Lemmy casually responded, 'Oh, call me back later,' and promptly fell back asleep. Waking once more, five minutes later, he was convinced that the whole experience was merely a dream.

On Motörhead's cult appeal

'I'm sure we're gonna be like Van Gogh, who couldn't sell a painting while he was alive. And then we're gone and everybody will be queuing up to buy.' **2000**

'It's not that I take pride in being unfashionable. It's just that I've gotten used to it. I do it rather well now. I've been practising for a long time.' **1996**

'Whether people like us or not is not important. I think we're necessary. I think you deserve us.' **2002**

'I can see three generations out there any time we play. Where else could a 63-year-old fucked-up c**t like me get an audience like that?' **2009**

. . .

On whether Motörhead are still dangerous

'I think we used to be. But we still do all right; you better be cautious around us. We still have one tooth, and it's very sharp.' **1994**

'Don't come on my stage or I'll fucking cripple ya! I am not responsible once I am onstage. If you come on my stage you risk your own life.' **1998**

. . .

On life without Motörhead

'I'd be in jail. No contest. I'd be in the furthest one down on the left, next to Hannibal Lecter.' **1998**

. . .

15

THINKING OUT LOUD

On the perks of the job

'I get to travel all over the world, I get to
sleep with women of all colours and religious
persuasions and I get to play the music I like
and make people happier than they were
when I arrived. It's a good way to make a
living. You find me a better one.' **2005**

'I only care about my band and all the rest of
you can go fuck yourselves.' **2008**

.   .   .

And don't forget the joker . . .

'I've got what's called a Low Tonal Register
which, loosely translated, means I sound like
a gorilla on Valium.' **2004**

Lemmy's Early Days

Lemmy's life less ordinary began in Burslem, a tough working class town in Stoke-on-Trent, England. Born Ian Fraser Kilmister on Christmas Eve 1945, he was just three months old when his father, a former Royal Air Force chaplain, walked out on the family. Raised initially by his mother and grandmother, before his mother remarried and relocated the family to Wales, young Lemmy quickly developed a stubborn independent streak and a healthy disrespect for authority. Expelled from school before he could gain any qualifications, he was fired from his first proper job – at a Hotpoint washing machine factory – for refusing to get his hair cut. A normal life was never really on the cards . . .

. . .

On his earliest memory
'It's standing in my cot, shaking the bars, shouting. I was probably rehearsing.' **2000**

. . .

On his upbringing
'I come from a broken home. I broke it.' **2004**

'They [Lemmy's mother and father] were young when they got married, at the end of the war, the whole wartime romance thing. She was probably struck by his uniform and his holiness, he was probably struck by her legs and her ass.' **2007**

'I had a very good childhood. My mother worked like a bastard and she did a good job. I learned to be honourable and to live and let live and to be upright and strong as she was.' **2002**

. . .

On his infamous warts

'My mother always told me they were beauty spots, but I knew.'

2000

. . .

THINKING OUT LOUD

On his schooldays

'All I learned at school was how to dodge fighting and how to smoke. And what girls' tits looked like.' **2004**

'I was the only English kid in a school of 700 Welsh kids. That's when I learned that fighting was pointless, because there's always someone who's gonna come along and tie your legs up in a knot behind your head.' **1990**

. . .

Never shy about expressing his lack of interest in school, Lemmy finally broke the patience of his teachers after being caught playing truant at age 15. He was summoned to the headmaster's office and instructed to prepare for the cane. As he had a barely healed penknife cut on one finger, Lemmy asked if he could receive the strokes on his other hand. The headmaster refused and brought his cane down sharply on Lemmy's injured hand, sending blood spurting across the room. Big mistake. 'I took the cane off him and smacked him round the head with it,' Lemmy recalled in 1998. He was immediately expelled. 'If any kids want advice on how to get out of school early, that'll do it.'

. . .

On his first love, horses

'Horses make women horny. There's a sexual power to a horse.' **2002**

'Horses are brute force and women aren't. If you treated a horse like you treated a woman he'd stamp on your foot. And if you treated a woman like you treated a horse she'd leave. I could probably still make her walk sideways though.' **2008**

'Horses are the only animal with a sense of
humour.' **1998**

'I was gonna be a horse breaker;
that was my dream. And then I
heard Little Richard and literally
that was it. I thought, "That
sounds great. He sounds like he's
really having a fucking good
time." And then I learned there
were women connected to it as
well. So that was it.' **2002**

. . .

On working at the Hotpoint factory

'My [step-] father got me a job at the Hotpoint factory to show me what the real values of life were. And the real values of life were discussing football and reading the *Daily Mirror* every fucking day, so I thought I'd get some new values.' **2002**

'Ever since I left that job I've appreciated every day I'm not in it. I could feel it rotting my mind. Any intelligence would drive you nuts. You knock yourself down intellectually to cope.' **1998**

. . .

On his step-father

'I never really got into that father-son mode – "Let's go and kill something small and furry, son, and prove we're men!"' **2009**

. . .

On his one and only meeting with his father as an adult

'He kept writing to me saying he was full of remorse about his "boy"'. He couldn't even remember my fucking name.' **2000**

'He was a mealy-mouthed little shit. Not good enough. Bring me another one.' **2002**

. . .

And don't forget the joker . . .

'I didn't always have the moustache, I've only had that since I was 11.' **2002**

Lemmy on
Rock 'n' Roll

In March 1958, Lemmy's stepfather took him to see rock 'n' roll pioneer Buddy Holly on his first, and only, UK tour. Remarkably, like rock's very own Forrest Gump, Lemmy has been present at the birth of every significant guitar-based musical trend since. He saw the Beatles at the Cavern Club. He used to crash out at Rolling Stone Ronnie Wood's mum's house. He roadied for Jimi Hendrix, and was actually due to audition for the legendary guitarist's band on the day Hendrix died. He taught the Sex Pistols' Sid Vicious how to play the bass guitar . . . or rather tried to. In later years his band Motörhead have inspired rock superstars

THINKING OUT LOUD

Guns N' Roses, Metallica and Nirvana. And at 63 years of age, Lemmy still refuses to go quietly into the night . . .

. . .

'I am rock and roll and rock and roll is me.'
2001

. . .

On his career choice
'I watched this TV programme, and there was Eddie Cochran and Gene Vincent and Cliff Richard. And they were surrounded by screaming women. And I thought: that's the job for me.' **2004**

. . .

On Cliff Richard
'He was the mean, moody one. He was our Elvis.' **2009**

'I just like to be loud and shout
and run around. Rock 'n' roll
should be Saturday night every
night.' **1982**

'I don't really admire musicianship, per se –
as is obvious from my own playing. I don't
want to watch four guys playing their
instruments and looking at their shoes. But I
do admire a good act. I want to see people
from another planet. I want to see people
come down and speak to me for an hour
and a half and go away again – in the magic
spacecraft. I went to see Gene Vincent, and
he was definitely from another planet. And
that's as it should be.' **2004**

. . .

On Little Richard

'Little Richard is directly responsible for
Motörhead. I heard "Good Golly Miss Molly"
and that was the end of it.' **1996**

'Elvis inspired my sideburns, but Little
Richard inspired me for vocals. He had the
purest, most joyous rock 'n' roll voice.' **2009**

'He was the king and queen of rock 'n' roll.' **2009**

'I never met Little Richard. I don't want to
meet him now, because he's had it. I've seen
him play live in the last four or five years and
he's no good anymore, he can still do it, but
he doesn't do it, he sits there telling stories
and hands out Bibles. This is not what I
came to see!' **2009**

. . .

On Jimi Hendrix

'Hendrix was the most startling guitarist ever, no doubt about that. Everything about him was great – his playing was truly astounding, plus he had a great stage act. He was like a cat, a snake! When he performed he would drive the chicks fucking nuts. I've seen him go into his bedroom with five chicks – and they'd all come out smiling too.' **2002**

'With Hendrix, everything turned Technicolor. He stunned everybody – musicians, audiences. He'd go out on stage and it was, like, "Yes, The Messiah has spoken."' **2007**

'We didn't cluster around his kneecaps gazing adoringly and waiting for pearls of wisdom to fall from his lips. We were taking acid all the time and getting fucked up.' **2007**

'He'd just walk on stage and people would go: "Ahhh." Even on his bad nights. A lot of the time Hendrix was rubbish, the worst stuff you'd ever heard in your life. He'd be out of tune, stompin' on his fuzz box. He'd be terrible. But he'd still command.' **1999**

On the enduring power of rock 'n' roll

'They keep trying to kiss off rock 'n' roll. When rap came in, that was the death of rock 'n' roll again, right? When emo came in, when new wave came in, when punk came in, that was all the death of rock 'n' roll. It's really funny, over the years, to watch it go by. Rock 'n' roll always rears its ugly head again.' **2008**

'Rock 'n' roll deserves to be kept alive and we're some of the only motherfuckers that seem to care.' **1998**

After a poor performance in a Channel 4 'How rock 'n' roll are you?' test

'I don't need Channel 4 to tell me how rock 'n' roll I am; I'm in fucking Motörhead!'

'Forget art and all that – that's bullshit. If you can send that shiver down a kid's back then that's what it's all about. All else is bullshit. That's what rock 'n' roll was for in the first place and as far as I'm concerned that's what it's still about. I'm trying to give them that feeling I felt the first time I heard "All Shook Up" or "Good Golly Miss Molly". I just want to send that shiver up their back because it's the best thing I ever felt. It's better than screwing.' **1979**

· · ·

On the suggestion that he's too old to rock

'I'm not too old, and until I decide I'm too old I'll never be too fucking old.' **2005**

THINKING OUT LOUD

'Someone said to me recently that I should retire and make room for some young ones and I said, "Fuck you! I haven't seen anyone better than me, so why should I jack it in?" People think rock 'n' roll is all about teenage rebellion, but why can't there be old rebels as well?' **2007**

'Getting to travel around the world and bring joy to people is not the worst job in the world. It's better than spraying napalm on children, and they give you a medal for that.' **1996**

. . .

And don't forget the joker . . .
'A girlfriend of mine once fucked Mick Jagger. I asked her what he was like, and she said, "Well, he was good, but he was no Jagger!"' **1997**

Lemmy on Sex

In 2008 Chicago toy company Lococo announced their intention to produce a Lemmy action figure, replete with a miniature Rickenbacker bass and angled microphone stand. The man himself complained that the figure was not anatomically complete. 'They said it's an action figure, and I said, "Are you gonna put a dick on it?" and they said, "No." I said, "Well, it's not gonna get much action then, is it?"'

Happily for Lemmy, this has never been a problem in real life. In June 2006 *Maxim* magazine placed him in their Top 10 Living Legends of Sex list (alongside such luminaries as actor Jack Nicholson, singer Julio Iglesias and Kiss bassist Gene

Simmons), and while he scoffed at magazine claims that he's slept with over 2,000 women, insisting that his total would be closer to just 1,000, he conceded: 'It could be more, because I only remember the pretty ones.'

. . .

'I like girls. That's the only reason I'm in the music business – I discovered you could get women to take their clothes off if you had a guitar. And they come off a lot faster if you can play it.' **1991**

'I've been a slut all my life. Who's happier than a slut?' **2002**

'Sex is the most fun you can have without laughing.'

. . .

On losing his virginity

'My first shag was fucking disastrous. But I've made up for it since. I was 13. You don't know what the fuck you're doing, you're just hoping for the best and diving in there. It was on a beach as well. That fucking sand gets everywhere, even under your foreskin.' **1998**

. . .

On his youthful appetite for sex

'I had to beat the fucking thing with a hammer to get it to go down at one point. Those days are gone.' **1996**

. . .

'When you're younger, you'll sell your soul to the devil for some pussy, but you get over that. You don't have to be special to get my interest now.' **2009**

. . .

On the difficulty of maintaining a relationship while in a rock 'n' roll band

'It's not an ideal job for an enduring, committed, caring relationship, because on the road your main objective is to get fucked all the time: in the back of the bus, under the bus, on top of the bus . . . And given that, the bird feels a bit uneasy when you're away for three months.' **1998**

'To have a relationship is fatal to the relationship.'

. . .

Motörhead's 'Rules of the Road'
'Two legs good, four legs bad.' **2008**

. . .

On 'groupies'

'There is no such thing as a groupie. There are girls that like to fuck and girls that don't.' **2002**

'If a woman likes you, you're not bothered why they like you. I'm really shallow like that. People say, "Doesn't it bother you that they just want you because you're famous?" And I say, "No. Never did. Ever. Not for one second." They can have me. I'm a whore, always was. In fact they don't even have to pay me.' **2004**

'I chase women when I'm on the road, and when I'm not on the road I just chase women. Catch a few, too.' **2006**

'Famous people get all the chicks. I don't get them now as I'm just too old but I had a good innings. I had my share. And yours too.' **2008**

. . .

On being asked if he practises safe sex

'Yeah. We sit at opposite ends of the room and shout "Fuck you!" at each other.' **1995**

'I had the clap seven times in two years, '66 and '67, and then I haven't had it since. I think I'm immune.' **1996**

. . .

On his fondness for strip clubs

'I've never seen the point in denying the fact that I enjoy looking at naked girls.' **2007**

. . .

On whether or not porn stars are better in bed than 'regular' women

'No, they're just the same, but then again I'm not as good in bed as the people I usually fuck, so I suppose it evens out.' **2009**

'How does a real man know when a woman's having an orgasm? Real men don't care . . .' **1996**

. . .

'I love women. I think they should be naked backstage all the time.'

. . .

THINKING OUT LOUD

Answering the question 'Who's gagging for a shagging?'

'I would like to have fucked Madonna before she had the kid. The tits go south, don't they?' **1998**

. . .

On the onset of AIDS

'AIDS wasn't a wake-up call. It was a go-to-sleep call.' **2004**

In a 1995 interview about his attitude to sex, Lemmy stressed, 'I don't kiss and tell. I don't nudge people in the ribs and say, "Guess who I did last night."' Unfortunately, not everyone shares this noble moral stance. In 2000, Playboy model Julie Watson told British tabloid *The People*, 'Lemmy once tied me to the bed for three days . . . it was an incredible session.' Naturally, the singer was mortified, and called in his lawyers. 'Our client wishes to protest furiously,' the legal eagles solemnly stated. 'It wasn't three days. It was two weeks and she was hanging from the ceiling!'

.   .   .

On homosexuality

'If I fancied it I'd try it – I don't give a fuck – but I've never fancied it. I've got enough trouble getting round all the chicks I fancy, let alone starting on the geezers.' **1992**

.   .   .

To an internet journalist who claimed that he is bisexual

'How will you be able to go out and buy new floppy discs when you have a screwdriver through both knees?' **2006**

THINKING OUT LOUD

'I prefer extended foreplay. You can make foreplay last for 48 hours if you're really careful.' **1997**

'I'm a blow job fan. Ever since I found out about it I couldn't believe that everybody didn't do it all the time.' **1996**

. . .

On Viagra

'I still use it, now and again. If Percy isn't pointing at the pulchritude then he needs a bit of a push.' **2007**

. . .

And don't forget the joker . . .

'I've never gone to bed with an ugly chick, but I've woken up with a few.' **2006**

Lemmy on Excess

In 1973 rumours spread that, in order to avoid the pain of detoxing, Rolling Stones guitarist Keith Richards had checked himself into a Swiss clinic to replace his blood supply with untainted, fresh blood. Though Richards would later dismiss the story, it had gained sufficient notoriety within the music industry that by 1980 Lemmy, a long term, hugely committed advocate of the use of acid and speed, was considering undertaking the process. His doctor, however, had other ideas. Pure blood, Lemmy was told, would kill him. And his own blood was considered so toxic that it would kill the average man. Almost 30 years on however, Lemmy's

thirst for excess remains unquenchable,
leading fellow *bon vivant* Ozzy Osbourne to
note, 'If an atom bomb fell there would be
three survivors: cockroaches, Keith
Richards and Lemmy.'

. . .

On the irony of his exit from Hawkwind
'Being fired from Hawkwind for drugs is a bit
like being pushed off the Empire State
Building for liking heights.' **1999**

. . .

On his love of Jack Daniel's bourbon
'I try to do a bottle a day. Whether I need it
or not.' **1998**

. . .

On absinthe

'It feels quite benign until you find yourself on a balcony at four in the morning with a pistol, stark naked.' **2009**

. . .

On the idea of staying sober for a day

'I did that once in 1975. I didn't like it.' **2005**

. . .

On 'lost' days

'That was a great time, the summer of '71. I can't remember it, but I'll never forget it!'

. . .

THINKING OUT LOUD

On acid

'Acid made me a better person.' **2003**

'Orgasms on acid are fucking excellent.' **2002**

'Acid gives you a new angle on things. Several new angles. I wouldn't undo having done it. I've only ever had one bad trip, which was given to me by this asshole . . . Whatever you do, don't look in the mirror. All the flesh melts off your face. And you are sick forever. But I took another one the next day, you know, just to get on the horse.' **2004**

In 1973, Lemmy's then-girlfriend Susan
Bennett died after taking an accidental
overdose of heroin. She was 19 years old.
The tragedy served to strengthen Lemmy's
hatred of the drug – he once turned in a
heroin dealer to the police – and he has
spoken out against its use ever since. In
2005 the singer was invited by Conservative
MP William Graham to address the Welsh
assembly on the dangers of the drug. To the
MP's surprise, and presumably horror,
Lemmy used the occasion to advocate that
heroin should be legalised in order to allow
its use to be regulated and taxed. 'Lemmy
certainly has an alternative solution to the
one presently being tried,' Graham noted
afterwards.

THINKING OUT LOUD

On heroin

'It degrades you, makes you a slobbering animal, it also makes you easy prey and it kills you. It takes away everything, your dignity, your job, it's just a fucking disgusting horrible thing.' **1986**

'It stops you from taking care of business. It stops your breathing too. People don't understand that because they think people who are older than them know nothing. We're all just old, dumb and finished. They're the new, brave, young breed and it won't happen to them. They think they're smarter but heroin is smarter than everybody.' **1996**

'If I saw a smack dealer on the street I'd shoot the fucking c**t.' **1986**

On the glamorisation of heroin by rock stars

'Heroin fucking ruined him [Keith Richards] for years. It's all very well, that funky Keith business, but how many people do you think he influenced? All these young guys impressed by Keith and doing it as well. You've got to take some kind of fucking responsibility.' **2004**

'Lou Reed should burn in hell for the amount of people he's got into heroin through that song ["Heroin"].' **1999**

On just saying 'No'

'I truly believe that if you can do without them [drugs] then you're better off. I hate to give advice because I'm 53 – I'm their parents' age – so they think, "What's that old c**t know?" But I do know, believe me. I fucking know.' **1999**

THINKING OUT LOUD

On his cast iron constitution

'I got checked over in Berlin two weeks ago and my doctor said I have got the liver of a new-born baby. I'm sure everybody who's switched to fucking nut cutlets is really pissed off by that.' **2006**

'I don't recommend my lifestyle. It's been finely tuned over a long time. It would kill most people.' **1998**

. . .

And don't forget the joker . . .

'I don't get hangovers. You have to stop drinking to get a hangover. Why stop?' **2002**

Lemmy vs the Music Industry

Few bands are less interested in playing the corporate game than Motörhead. In 1992, when the band were nominated in the Best Metal Performance category at the Grammy Awards for their 1916 album, it was a rare gesture of acknowledgement from a hipper-than-thou music industry which has largely sought to keep the band at a safe, respectable distance. Given that his band have been ripped off, dismissed and patronised within the industry for decades, Lemmy viewed the accolade – and the ceremony itself – with a certain amount of wry detachment, witheringly observing: 'Everyone was dressed in hired penguin tuxedos, trying to look as much as possible like the motherfuckers who were stealing their money.'

. . .

'We don't play the game,' Lemmy snorted. 'I had a great speech ready in the event we had won. I was going to say, "I'm not going to thank anybody. None of you fuckers have ever given us a hand. You didn't do anything."'

. . .

Sadly the assembled suits never got to hear the speech, as Motörhead lost out on the night to Metallica's self-titled fifth album. Ironically when they did finally win a Grammy, in 2005, they did so not with a Motörhead original, but with a cover version of a Metallica song, 'Whiplash'. It's little wonder that Lemmy views the industry with such contempt.

'I always take notice of what people say, but I'd rather talk to any two kids in the street than any ten people in the record business.' 1983

. . .

THINKING OUT LOUD

On musicians who preach

'You get musicians going, "I have a message for the kids." Well bollocks to that. I didn't have a message for the kids, except for the female kids, where my message was: "Come round backstage."' **2000**

'Look at those assholes the Clash calling their album *Sandinista*. What the fuck do they know about hard times? They live in England, they don't have hard times in England like they do in Nicaragua. That's a cheap shot.' **1986**

. . .

On fame

'People work for all of three years to get famous, then they are and then they say they can't fucking stand it. Well fuck off then and make room for someone that can fucking stand it!' **2000**

. . .

On giving speeches at awards ceremonies
'I should get up there and just tell the truth when I give out the next award: "Here is an asshole who is taking your money on false pretences and he's getting the award on the unanimous decision of all these c**ts who never buy records and get into gigs for free."'
2003

. . .

**To a journalist who expressed a
preference for Lloyd Webber musicals over
rock music**

'You should be nailed to the fucking cross.'

2004

. . .

On heavy metal

'I never listened to heavy metal, even when it
wasn't called heavy metal. I always found it
too slow, too ponderous, too pompous.'

2000

'Heavy metal is people who shriek and plod
around.' **1997**

'People call us heavy metal because we have
long hair. If we had short hair, they would've
called us punk. They just look at the surface,
the clothes; they didn't want to look at what
we really do.' **1997**

𝕷𝖊𝖒𝖒𝖞 VS THE MUSIC INDUSTRY

On Ozzy Osbourne

'Ozzy was a nice guy, still is. Very twisted, but nice. Of course you're going to be a bit warped when people are throwing half a dozen doves with broken legs and wings on stage every time you play a gig.' **2002**

. . .

On the Beatles

'I saw the Beatles several times and they were the best band I ever saw live by a long, long way. They had this amazing confidence – they would walk on stage exuding this power. They presented themselves as the best gang in the world and you believed them.' **2008**

. . .

THINKING OUT LOUD

On the Rolling Stones

'I did like the Stones, but they were never anywhere near the Beatles – not for humour, not for originality, not for songs, not for presentation. All they had was Mick Jagger dancing about. Fair enough, the Stones made great records, but they were always shit onstage, whereas the Beatles were the gear.' **2002**

. . .

On Foo Fighters' frontman Dave Grohl

'I like Dave a lot, Dave is one of nature's true gentlemen. Some guys you meet in this business manage to get through it without becoming an asshole, which is an achievement really.' **2008**

. . .

On the Sex Pistols

'I remember thinking that Johnny Rotten was a terrible singer. He couldn't sing in tune. But I got past that, and then I realised he didn't want to be in tune. He had my wholehearted support after that, because that's what I've been trying to do all these years!' **2000**

. . .

On pro-hunting 'Motor City Madman' Ted Nugent

'I don't think running around the woods in a loincloth killing deer with a bow and arrow makes you more of a man.' **1997**

. . .

THINKING OUT LOUD

On Limp Bizkit

'It's all crap . . . sorry, sorry Fred. We did
Ozzfest with him. Not good enough. In the
'70s he would have been bottled off the
stage.' **1998**

. . .

On Kid Rock

'Fucking Kid Rock. "I am rock 'n' roll." No
you're not, man. If you have to have a dwarf
onstage it's kind of rough isn't it? His dwarf
died so he's going to have to go down into
the woods to the cottage again and find
another fucker. It's fucking pathetic.' **2001**

. . .

On modern bands

'New bands now are a bunch of bed-wetters. The music is full of complaining and whining. Music used to be happy, now it's all doom and pity. They are all sell-outs and out for the quick buck.'

2002

'They play angry music and live on the computer. It should be about the music and getting laid, not the computer. I know how to tour and it does not include a laptop. These guys need to learn that real men don't type, they fuck on the road. They should become secretaries if they want to type.' **2002**

. . .

THINKING OUT LOUD

One modern band with whom Lemmy does
have an affinity is San Franciscan metal
superstars Metallica, whose drummer Lars
Ulrich was once in charge of Motörhead's
American fan club. One quiet drinking night
for Lemmy and Ulrich in the early '80s saw
the drummer pass out, covered in his own
vomit, in his hero's LA hotel room. A typically
unsympathetic Lemmy took photos of the
hapless puke-covered Dane and used one
on a subsequent Motörhead album sleeve.

Such japes did nothing to diminish Ulrich's
fan-boy worship. Indeed, on 14 December
1995 Metallica – now firmly established as
the world's biggest rock band – donned wigs
and mutton-chops and scrawled 'Ace of
Spades' tattoos on their forearms to play
Lemmy's 50th birthday in Los Angeles as a
Motörhead tribute band called The Lemmys.
'That was the biggest compliment anybody

has ever paid me,' Lemmy said, though the gruff old bugger still found room for complaint: 'They got their tattoos on the wrong arm, every one of them.'

On his iconic status within rock 'n' roll

'I don't want to be a fuckin' legend. I want to be a competitor.' **2002**

'I can never be anonymous – especially when I walk round looking like this; especially when I take so much trouble not to be anonymous, right? It means it's working. I mean, if you're a rock star, you should bloody well be a rock star, and stop fucking around.' **2004**

'There's a lot of people slicing bacon and making car parts for a living who were better musicians than me. I just persevered.' **2000**

. . .

And don't forget the joker . . .

'Courtney Love? What a fucking horse! I wouldn't fuck her with a stolen dick!' 1997

Lemmy vs 'The Man'

A psychologist might point to the absence of a male authority figure in Lemmy's childhood as a root cause of his lifelong distrust and dislike of 'The Man' – teachers, the police, politicians, religious leaders; pretty much anyone in a uniform. Perhaps surprisingly, though, given his outlaw swagger and reputation for pharmaceutical excess, Lemmy's criminal record is remarkably slim, boasting only a couple of minor drug busts and a slightly laughable 'possession of an offensive weapon' charge dating back to the early '70s when he was caught with a penknife bearing the inscription 'Present from Norway' on the handle. 'Real heavy stuff,' as the man himself once noted. Still, the experiences clearly still rankle: 'The only thing I'm prejudiced against is the record business. And the police of course,' Lemmy once spat. 'Put your trust in those bastards? I fucking hate them.'

. . .

On politicians

'I don't agree with any politician. I think they're all c**ts. Tony fucking smiley Blair – he's just the same c**t as the last c**t. His suit's different, that's all.' **1998**

𝕷𝖊𝖒𝖒𝖞 VS 'THE MAN'

'I'm asked why I don't get involved in politics. The answer is: because all politicians are bastards. I don't trust any of those idiots. The louder they scream, the more stupid they are.' **2004**

'I think all politicians are arseholes, by definition. The fact that they wanted to be a politician speaks volumes about them. What kind of person must you be to want to kiss other people's babies? Fuck, you don't even want to kiss your own babies.' **2005**

'I didn't like Bill Clinton and I don't like George Bush. I didn't like Eisenhower either. I liked John Kennedy, but only because he didn't have time to fuck up.' **2001**

THINKING OUT LOUD

'What the fuck is a social conscience? The bastards with the money always win in the end.' **1999**

.   .   .

On Britain's royal family
'I believe in the royal family. They may be blockheads, some of them, but at least they're trained blockheads.' **2004**

'The Queen was a really cute chick when she was still a princess – her and Princess Margaret were both really horny.'
1999

.   .   .

The bane of Lemmy's life has been politically correct liberals accusing him of having far right sympathies, a result of misinterpretations of Lemmy's self-confessed fascination with World War II, and his penchant for collecting valuable art and memorabilia from the period. His habit of frequently sporting an Iron Cross and Nazi caps hasn't helped. As recently as July 2008, the *Guardian* newspaper reported that Lemmy could face prosecution in Germany for wearing a Nazi cap in a newspaper photo shoot ('anti-constitutional symbols', including Nazi souvenirs, being illegal under the German penal code).

The subject has been a source of irritation for Lemmy for decades. 'If people looked at my actions and deeds over the years rather than something I collect they would see I couldn't possibly be a Nazi,' he seethed in 2000. 'If I was going to be a Nazi I would write songs with Nazi sympathies. I have no sympathy with any political persuasion whatsoever, probably the least with Nazism and Communism, which I regard as the same thing under a different flag. I'm disgusted that people who've known me for a long time have started coming up to me and asking me if I have Nazi sympathies when they should've fucking known better.'

. . .

𝕷𝖊𝖒𝖒𝖞 VS 'THE MAN'

On his fascination with World War II

'It's the most important event of the 20th
Century. If you're not interested in it, you're
sort of an idiot. It contained every lesson
you'll ever need to work with today. And yet
people will not learn from past events. They
keep on making the same mistakes every
fucking time. It's incredible. We have an
unlimited capacity for stupidity.' **2005**

. . .

**On his extensive collection of
WWII uniforms**

'From the beginning of time, the bad guys
always had the best uniforms. Napoleon, the
Confederates, the Nazis. They all had killer
uniforms. I mean, the SS uniform is fucking
brilliant! They were the rock stars of that time.
What you gonna do? They just look good.'
2007

'People like war because it (a) gets them away from the wife; (b) they get to exercise their frustrations on people with a gun; (c) people love parades.' **2000**

. . .

On Hitler

'Hitler is an interesting man. The trouble is that people don't realise he was only a man. He wasn't a monster, he wasn't made by symbiosis, he was a man, like everybody else. And that's the trouble, because when you realise that, then you have to examine yourself, 'cause he came from the same gene pool you came from. If you put him in the 'Monster' box it's too easy.' **2000**

'Hitler was a magnetic speaker, and he came out of nowhere to take over a country he didn't live in. As a person, though, he was so boring — a vegetarian, no smoking or drinking. And a short haircut . . .' **1997**

'The Americans killed more people [Native Americans] than Hitler, it's just that they didn't have any relatives on Wall Street to write to *The Times* about it.' **1983**

. . .

On big business

'We're done. Pretty soon we'll all either be extinct or living in hermetically sealed caves because we're poisoning the air we breathe, we're poisoning the water we drink, we're poisoning the food we eat. Any questions? And it's not like we haven't known this, but businesses wanted the money more than they wanted their children to live. Isn't that wonderful? You can count on mankind every time.' **2009**

. . .

'Safe sex, safe music, safe clothing, safe hair spray, safe ozone layer. Too late! Everything that's been achieved in the history of mankind has been achieved by not being safe.'

. . .

And don't forget the joker . . .

'The only thing we've learned in 2000 years of civilisation is how to kill more people from further away, so we don't have to see it.'

1999

Lemmy vs God

Given that his vicar father walked out on his family when Lemmy was just three months old, it's hardly surprising that Lemmy grew up with a rather jaundiced view of organised religion and the church ('a fashion show for fags'). This was only exacerbated when the Catholic Church would agree to his devoutly religious stepfather marrying his divorcee mother only if Lemmy was declared illegitimate. In latter years Lemmy summed up his attitude to religion in a 2004 Channel 4 documentary on Motörhead titled *Live Fast Die Old* with the unequivocal comment, 'Fuck God and fuck the Devil.'

'I'm very Buddha, me, I sit and watch the shit go by.' **1999**

'Having a vicar for a father isn't easy. Someone's always trying to baptise you. I had to fight tooth and nail to stop them.' **1983**

'I dislike religion quite intensely. It's been the cause of all the grief in the world ever since they discovered the first stone to worship.' **2002**

'I don't worship anything but rock 'n' roll.' **1986**

.   .   .

On the Virgin Birth

'A virgin impregnated by a ghost? If Joseph believes that he deserves to be in a stable.'
2002

. . .

On Jesus

'I thought he was really well-adjusted for an only child.' **2006**

. . .

On God

'If there is a God he hasn't been paying attention. He should retire and hand over to a younger man, because he's making a real bollocks of everything.' **2002**

. . .

THINKING OUT LOUD

On The Bible
'The Bible is some book! Fucking sex and violence all the way through it!' **2007**

. . .

On alternative religions
'Christians can't help themselves. Fucking Hare Krishnas are the worst. You want me to look like that? Ha ha ha, maybe next year . . .' **1986**

. . .

On the wrath of God
'Thank you, oh Lord, for the gift of AIDS to teach us a fucking lesson. Just when we all had our pants down, enjoying ourselves, bingo. Sometimes I think God would have made a wonderful Pope.' **2002**

There's a scene in Adam Sandler's hugely forgettable 1994 film comedy *Airheads* where, playing hair-brained heavy metal musicians Chazz and Rex, Brendan Fraser and Steve Buscemi ask another character: 'Who'd win in a wrestling match, Lemmy or God?' The unfortunate hostage first says, 'Lemmy,' then, 'God.' 'Wrong, dickhead,' says Buscemi's character, Rex. 'Trick question, Lemmy *is* God.'

. . .

On Hell

'I'm going down there, because that's where all the pool tables are.' **2006**

. . .

THINKING OUT LOUD

On people who claim 'The Devil made me do it . . .'

'Fuck Satan, you're responsible for your own deeds. *You're* responsible for your own mistakes. And it's your responsibility to leave the world a better place than when you came into it for your passage through it. That's what you're supposed to do. It's not about God or the Devil.' **2000**

. . .

And don't forget the joker . . .

'A geezer last night said, "Lemmy, you're God!" I said, "No, I'm not, God's much taller!"' **2007**

Lemmy on Life... and Death

In 2007 a columnist for the *Guardian's* website dubbed Lemmy 'the Nation's Greatest Living Englishman', noting, 'He may have hit many a duff note in the past 30 years, but the man behind "Ace of Spades" has not once told you a lie.' A fair point, well made. Both an old school gentleman *and* an unapologetically unreconstructed male, Lemmy has never been one to pull punches, and his considered opinions on life, love and liberty are always delivered forcefully and with sincerity, just daring you to argue. Principled, philosophical and frequently poetic, he's quite the master of the carefully chosen apophthegm. As another

THINKING OUT LOUD

Guardian writer once noted, 'If he didn't swear so much, he would be an excellent addition to the panel on *Question Time*.'

. . .

'Despite my appearance, believe me, I am a gentleman.' **2002**

'My ethic is: "Eat, drink and be merry, for tomorrow we die." You can be as careful as you want, but you're gonna die anyway, so why not have fun?' **2009**

'You treat me like a human being and I'll treat you the same – otherwise you can just fuck off. You can have either: you can have the nice guy or you can have the c**t – you choose it.' **2005**

'I've never done anything for a bet. Fuck 'em, I ain't cheap entertainment for anybody.' **1998**

'I'm quite quiet offstage. I think I'm really bloody boring, but apparently I'm not, because chicks keep coming back. I must be doing something right.' **1996**

'It's much more fun to be full of hope than pessimism.' **2009**

'We can't have everything 'cause where would we put it?' **2004**

'It's not important where you've been, it's where you're going that's important.'

. . .

On England

'It's never recognised any of its own talent, it's never done anything to promote anything but the status quo. It'll always be stuck with rotten politicians. England had a history once but now it's got nothing.' **2005**

'The British are resentful. They still haven't got over losing India. The British get on my tits all the time.'

2004

On his decision to quit England for LA

'The weather is better, the sun bounces down all year round, the girls wear a lot less clothes and everything is half the price. Any questions?' **2007**

'I like it here because you don't get the cynical fucking English bitching about everything. I find the Americans quite refreshing. Everybody sneers at the "Have a nice day" thing but it's a lot nicer than having your change thrown at you.' **2005**

. . .

On marriage

'I think marriage is very irrational. It was invented when we were all living in fucking mud huts.' **1998**

'I could never imagine looking at the same face over the cornflakes for the rest of my life. I don't know how people do it.' **2005**

'I used to say that getting married was the only mistake I didn't make,' Lemmy noted in 2004. But England's most confirmed bachelor since Cliff Richard hasn't managed to sow his wild oats entirely without consequence. Lemmy has two sons that he knows of, only one of whom is aware that Motörhead's frontman is his father, the other having been adopted at birth. 'His mother went up and found him,' Lemmy admitted in 2005. 'She said he put his head in his hands when she told him she was his mother so she hadn't the heart to tell [him] who his father was.'

. . .

On family

'I went out with a couple of girls with young babies. I can give a baby a bottle with one hand and roll a joint with the other, but I never wanted any of that. Changing nappies is horrible. Kids are generally rotten until the age of about six, when they become people.' **2005**

. . .

On mobile phones

'Hitler didn't have one and it didn't seem to slow him down.' **2001**

. . .

On the Internet

'It will either be the greatest thing that ever happened to us or the death of humanity. I am not sure which.' **1996**

. . .

THINKING OUT LOUD

And ten years on . . .

'The Internet is probably the greatest gift to mankind ever, and what do we use it for? Child porn. That's humanity for you.' **2006**

. . .

On his dietary habits

'I once stayed up for two weeks and all I had during that time was three blackcurrant pies and two yoghurts.' **1999**

'I don't have meals usually . . . I just eat sandwiches. My old guitarist Eddie Clark said I was the most inventive person he'd ever met with two slices of bread. Toasted sandwiches are great because you can stick spaghetti sauce in there, or mushy peas.'
2006

'I used to peel babies and roll them in salt now and again.' **2006**

. . .

On the possibility of retirement
'Why would I retire? I've got no grandchildren to dangle off my knee and I've got no rocking chair to rock on. I'm gonna carry on until I stop enjoying it and then I'll become a dirty old man.' **2007**

'Integrity is everything to me. I will not die ashamed. I will live on my deathbed knowing that I gave it my best shot and everything else is meaningless to me.' **2008**

'The day I die, then you can safely say that you won't see me onstage anymore. Unless they put me in a fucking jar . . .'

. . .

THINKING OUT LOUD

On death

'People don't become better when they are dead; you just talk about them as if they are. But it's not true. People are still assholes, they're just dead assholes.' **2002**

. . .

On his ideal funeral

'I'm going to have some pallbearers six foot six inches tall and some three foot two inches small. They'll carry me out in step to the Laurel and Hardy tune.' **2005**

. . .

Thank you and goodnight . . .

'I don't regret much. Fuck 'em.'

1996